C000136794

contents

Please note that Australian cup and
spoon measurements are metric.
A conversion chart appears on page 62.

poached pears in red wine syrup with pear crisps

6 medium pears (1.5kg)
2 cups (500ml) water
2 cups (500ml) dry red wine
½ cup (125ml) orange-
 flavoured liqueur
4 strips orange rind
¾ cup (165g) caster sugar
1 vanilla bean
pear crisps
1 medium pear (230g)
½ cup (110g) caster sugar
½ cup (125ml) water

1 Make pear crisps.
2 Meanwhile, peel pears, leaving stems intact.
3 Combine the water, wine, liqueur, rind and sugar in large saucepan. Split vanilla bean in half lengthways; scrape seeds into pan, place pod in pan. Stir over heat, without boiling, until sugar dissolves. Add pears; bring to the boil. Reduce heat; simmer, covered, about 1 hour or until pears are just tender.
4 Transfer pears to large bowl; bring syrup to the boil. Simmer, uncovered, about 10 minutes or until syrup reduces by a third. Remove from heat; discard pod.
5 Strain syrup over pears, cover; refrigerate 2 hours or until cold.
6 Divide pears and pear crisps among serving plates; drizzle with syrup.
pear crisps Preheat oven to 120°C/100°C fan-forced. Line oven tray with baking paper. Cut unpeeled pears into 2mm slices. Stir sugar and the water in saucepan over medium heat, without boiling, until sugar dissolves; bring to the boil. Boil, uncovered, about 5 minutes or until syrup thickens slightly. Add pear slices, reduce heat; simmer, uncovered, 5 minutes or until pear is just tender, drain. Arrange pear slices, in single layer, on oven tray. Bake in oven about 2 hours or until dried, turning occasionally. Cool 15 minutes or until crisp.

serves 6
preparation time 20 minutes
(plus refrigeration time)
cooking time 2 hours 15 minutes

orange and raspberry self-saucing pudding

¼ cup (20g) flaked almonds
30g butter
¾ cup (110g) self-raising flour
⅓ cup (80ml) milk
⅔ cup (150g) firmly packed brown sugar
2 teaspoons finely grated orange rind
¾ cup (110g) frozen raspberries
¼ cup (60ml) orange juice
¾ cup (180ml) boiling water

1 Grease shallow 1.5-litre (6-cup) microwave-safe dish.
2 Place nuts in small microwave-safe bowl; cook, uncovered, in microwave oven on HIGH (100%) about 2 minutes or until browned lightly.
3 Place butter in medium microwave-safe bowl; cook, uncovered, in microwave oven on HIGH (100%) 30 seconds. Add flour, milk and half the sugar; whisk until smooth. Stir in rind and raspberries; spread into dish.
4 Sprinkle remaining sugar over raspberry mixture; carefully pour combined juice and boiling water over mixture.
5 Place pudding on microwave-safe rack; cook, uncovered, in microwave oven on MEDIUM-HIGH (70%-80%) about 12 minutes. Stand 5 minutes.
6 Sprinkle pudding with nuts. Serve with cream or ice-cream, if desired.

serves 4
preparation time 5 minutes
cooking time 15 minutes
tips This recipe is best made close to serving. If cooking in a conventional oven, bake, uncovered, in moderately hot oven about 20 minutes.

coffee and pecan puddings with caramel sauce

¾ cup (90g) coarsely chopped roasted pecans
300ml cream
1½ cups (330g) firmly packed brown sugar
100g cold butter, chopped
125g butter, softened
1 teaspoon vanilla extract
½ cup (110g) caster sugar
2 eggs
1 cup (150g) self-raising flour
¼ cup (35g) plain flour
¼ cup (60ml) milk
1 tablespoon finely ground espresso coffee

1 Preheat oven to 180°C/160°C fan-forced. Grease six ¾-cup (180ml) ovenproof dishes; line bases with baking paper.
2 Divide nuts among moulds; place moulds on oven tray.
3 Stir cream, brown sugar and chopped butter in small saucepan over heat, without boiling, until sugar dissolves. Reduce heat; simmer, uncovered, without stirring, about 5 minutes or until mixture thickens slightly. Spoon 2 tablespoons of the sauce over nuts in each mould; reserve remaining sauce.
4 Beat softened butter, extract and caster sugar in small bowl with electric mixer until light and fluffy. Add eggs, one at a time, beating until just combined between additions. Stir in sifted flours, milk and coffee; divide mixture among moulds.
5 Bake, uncovered, in oven 30 minutes. Stand puddings 5 minutes before turning onto serving plates.
6 Reheat reserved sauce. Serve puddings with sauce, and cream or ice-cream, if desired.

serves 6
preparation time 15 minutes
cooking time 40 minutes
tip The caramel sauce and puddings can be made several hours ahead and reheated before serving.

lime meringue pie

250g plain sweet biscuits
100g unsalted butter, melted
½ cup (75g) wheaten cornflour
1½ cups (330g) caster sugar
½ cup (125ml) lime juice
1¼ cups (310ml) water
60g unsalted butter, extra
4 eggs, separated
2 teaspoons finely grated lime rind

1 Grease 24cm-round loose-based flan tin.
2 Blend or process biscuits until mixture resembles fine breadcrumbs.
Add butter; process until combined.
3 Press biscuit mixture evenly over base and 2cm up the side of tin; place
on oven tray. Refrigerate base while preparing filling.
4 Combine cornflour and ½ cup of the sugar in medium saucepan; gradually
stir in juice and the water until smooth. Cook, stirring, over high heat until
mixture boils and thickens. Reduce heat; simmer, stirring, 1 minute. Remove
from heat; stir in extra butter then yolks and rind. Continue stirring until
butter melts. Cool 10 minutes.
5 Spread filling over biscuit base; cover, refrigerate 2 hours.
6 Preheat oven to 200°C/180°C fan-forced.
7 Beat egg whites in small bowl with electric mixer until soft peaks form;
gradually add remaining sugar, 1 tablespoon at a time, beating until sugar
dissolves between additions.
8 Roughen surface of filling with a fork before spreading with meringue mixture.
Bake, uncovered, about 5 minutes or until meringue is browned lightly.

serves 10
preparation time 15 minutes (plus refrigeration time)
cooking time 15 minutes
tip The base and filling can be made and assembled up to one day ahead.

cinnamon flan

This recipe must be made 24 hours in advance to allow the toffee to dissolve.

1 cup (220g) caster sugar
½ cup (125ml) water
2½ cups (625ml) milk
300ml thickened cream
2 cinnamon sticks
2 whole cloves
4 eggs
2 egg yolks
⅓ cup (75g) caster sugar, extra
2 teaspoons vanilla extract

1 Preheat oven to 160°C/140°C fan-forced.

2 Stir sugar and the water in medium heavy-based saucepan over heat, without boiling, until sugar dissolves; bring to the boil. Reduce heat; simmer, uncovered, without stirring, until syrup is golden brown in colour. Pour syrup over base of deep 20cm-round cake pan. Place pan in large baking dish (toffee will set at this stage).

3 Combine milk, cream and spices in medium saucepan; bring to the boil. Remove from heat, cover; stand 15 minutes. Strain milk mixture; discard spices.

4 Whisk eggs, egg yolks, extra sugar and extract in medium bowl. Gradually whisk warm milk mixture into egg mixture; strain mixture over toffee in pan. Pour enough boiling water into baking dish to come halfway up side of pan.

5 Bake, uncovered, in oven about 45 minutes or until custard just sets. Remove pan from water; cool. Cover; refrigerate 24 hours.

6 Just before serving, turn flan onto a rimmed serving dish.

serves 8
preparation time 15 minutes
(plus standing and refrigeration time)
cooking time 1 hour

upside-down toffee banana cake

You need two large overripe bananas weighing about 460g to make 1 cup of mashed banana.

1 cup (220g) caster sugar
1 cup (250ml) water
2 medium bananas (400g), sliced thinly
2 eggs, beaten lightly
⅔ cup (160ml) vegetable oil
¾ cup (165g) firmly packed brown sugar
1 teaspoon vanilla extract
⅔ cup (100g) plain flour
⅓ cup (50g) wholemeal self-raising flour
2 teaspoons mixed spice
1 teaspoon bicarbonate of soda
1 cup mashed banana

1 Preheat oven to 180°C/160°C fan-forced. Grease deep 22cm-round cake pan; line base with baking paper.

2 Stir caster sugar and the water in medium saucepan over heat, without boiling, until sugar dissolves; bring to the boil. Boil, uncovered, without stirring, about 10 minutes or until golden in colour. Pour toffee into pan; top with sliced banana.

3 Combine eggs, oil, brown sugar and extract in medium bowl. Stir in sifted dry ingredients then mashed banana; pour mixture into pan.

4 Bake, uncovered, in oven about 40 minutes. Turn onto wire rack, peel off baking paper; turn cake top-side up. Serve cake warm or at room temperature with thick cream, if desired.

serves 8
preparation time 15 minutes
cooking time 55 minutes

vanilla cheesecake
with poached quinces

Granita biscuits are made from flour, wheat flakes, golden syrup, egg and malt, and their crumbly texture make them perfectly suitable as a cheesecake base.
This recipe must be started a day before serving.

125g Granita biscuits
80g butter, melted
1 vanilla bean, split in half
    lengthways
2 x 250g packets cream
    cheese, softened
2 eggs
½ cup (120g) sour cream
¼ cup (60ml) lemon juice
2⅔ cups (590g) caster sugar
2 cups (500ml) water
2 medium quinces (660g),
    peeled, cored, quartered
2 strips lemon rind

1   Preheat oven to 160°C/140°C fan-forced. Insert base of 23cm springform tin upside down in tin to give a flat base; grease tin.
2   Blend or process biscuits until mixture resembles fine breadcrumbs. Add butter; process until combined. Press biscuit mixture evenly over base of tin; cover, refrigerate about 30 minutes or until firm.
3   Meanwhile, scrape vanilla bean seeds into medium bowl; reserve pod for poached quinces. Add cream cheese, eggs, sour cream, juice and ⅔ cup of the sugar to seeds; beat with electric mixer until smooth.
4   Place tin on oven tray; pour in cheesecake mixture. Bake, uncovered, about 35 minutes or until set. Turn oven off; cool cheesecake in oven with door ajar. Cover cheesecake; refrigerate overnight.
5   The next day, stir the water and remaining sugar in medium saucepan over low heat until sugar dissolves. Add quince, rind and reserved vanilla pod; bring to the boil. Reduce heat; simmer, covered, about 2 hours or until quince is tender and rosy in colour. Cool quince in syrup, then slice thinly.
6   Return quince syrup to the boil. Reduce heat; simmer, uncovered, until syrup reduces by half; cool. Top cheesecake with quince slices; brush with syrup.

serves 12
preparation time 20 minutes
(plus refrigeration and cooling time)
cooking time 2 hours 45 minutes

crème brûlée

1 vanilla bean
3 cups (750ml) thickened cream
6 egg yolks
¼ cup (55g) caster sugar
¼ cup (40g) pure icing sugar

1 Preheat oven to 180°C/160°C fan-forced.
2 Split vanilla bean in half lengthways; scrape seeds into medium heatproof bowl. Heat pod and cream in medium saucepan without boiling.
3 Add egg yolks and caster sugar to seeds in bowl; gradually whisk in hot cream mixture. Place bowl over medium saucepan of simmering water; stir over heat about 10 minutes or until custard mixture thickens slightly and coats the back of a spoon. Discard pod.
4 Divide custard among six ½-cup (125ml) heatproof dishes. Place dishes in large baking dish; pour enough boiling water into baking dish to come halfway up sides of dishes. Bake, uncovered, in oven about 20 minutes or until custards just set. Remove custards from water; cool to room temperature. Cover; refrigerate 3 hours or overnight.
5 Preheat grill. Place custards in shallow flameproof dish filled with ice cubes; sprinkle custards evenly with sifted icing sugar. Using finger, spread the sugar evenly over the surface of each custard, pressing in gently; place under hot grill until tops are caramelised.

serves 6
preparation time 15 minutes (plus cooling and refrigeration time)
cooking time 40 minutes
tips Preheat grill on highest setting for about 5 minutes. It's important the icing sugar on the custards brown as quickly as possible (the ice in the baking dish helps keep the custards cold while the sugar is caramelising). You can also use a small blowtorch to melt then caramelise the icing sugar. Small blowtorches are available from hardware stores, some kitchenware shops and all professional cookware outlets.

chocolate brownie
with warm chocolate sauce

150g butter, chopped

300g dark eating chocolate, chopped coarsely

1½ cups (330g) firmly packed brown sugar

4 eggs, beaten lightly

1 cup (150g) plain flour

½ cup (120g) sour cream

½ cup (75g) roasted hazelnuts, chopped coarsely

warm chocolate sauce

150g dark eating chocolate, chopped coarsely

300ml thickened cream

⅓ cup (75g) firmly packed brown sugar

2 teaspoons coffee-flavoured liqueur

1 Preheat oven to 180°C/160°C fan-forced. Grease 20cm x 30cm lamington pan; line base and sides with baking paper.

2 Stir butter and chocolate in small saucepan over low heat until mixture is smooth. Transfer to medium bowl.

3 Stir sugar and eggs into chocolate mixture, then stir in flour, sour cream and nuts; spread mixture into pan. Bake, uncovered, in oven about 30 minutes. Cool in pan.

4 Meanwhile, make warm chocolate sauce.

5 Cut brownie into 16 pieces; serve drizzled with warm chocolate sauce, and scoops of vanilla ice-cream, if you like.

warm chocolate sauce Stir chocolate, cream and sugar in small saucepan over low heat until mixture is smooth. Remove from heat; stir in liqueur.

serves 8
preparation time 20 minutes
(plus cooling time)
cooking time 30 minutes
tip We used Kahlúa for this recipe but you can use any coffee-flavoured liqueur you like.

rhubarb and almond jalousie

You need approximately four large trimmed stalks of rhubarb for this recipe.

2 cups (250g) chopped rhubarb
⅓ cup (75g) caster sugar
2 sheets ready-rolled
  puff pastry
1 tablespoon apricot jam
1 egg white
1 tablespoon caster sugar,
  extra
frangipane filling
30g butter
¼ teaspoon vanilla extract
¼ cup (55g) caster sugar
1 egg
1 tablespoon plain flour
⅔ cup (80g) almond meal

1 Place rhubarb and sugar in medium saucepan; cook over low heat, stirring, until sugar dissolves and rhubarb softens.
2 Preheat oven to 200°C/180°C fan-forced. Grease oven tray.
3 Make frangipane filling.
4 Cut one pastry sheet into 14cm x 24cm rectangle; cut remaining pastry sheet into 16cm x 24cm rectangle. Leaving 2cm border around all sides, make about eight evenly spaced slits across width of larger pastry piece.
5 Place smaller pastry sheet on greased oven tray; spread with jam. Spread filling evenly over pastry, leaving 2cm border around the edges; top filling evenly with rhubarb mixture. Brush around border with egg white. Place remaining pastry sheet over filling; press edges of pastry together to seal.
6 Brush top of pastry with remaining egg white; sprinkle with extra sugar. Bake, uncovered, about 35 minutes or until jalousie is browned lightly and cooked through. Serve warm or cool with vanilla ice-cream, if desired.
frangipane filling Beat butter, vanilla and sugar in small bowl with electric mixer until thick and creamy. Add egg; beat until combined. Stir in flour and almond meal.

serves 8
preparation time 20 minutes
cooking time 40 minutes

sago plum puddings with orange cream

*Sago, also known as seed
or pearl tapioca, comes from
the sago palm and is used in
soups and desserts, and as
a thickening agent.*

2 cups (500ml) water
⅔ cup (130g) sago
1 teaspoon bicarbonate
    of soda
250g butter, softened
2 teaspoons vanilla extract
1 cup (220g) caster sugar
1 egg
½ cup (75g) plain flour
½ teaspoon bicarbonate
    of soda, extra
2 cups (140g) stale
    breadcrumbs
2 cups (320g) sultanas
orange cream
2 teaspoons finely grated
    orange rind
1 tablespoon orange-flavoured
    liqueur
1 tablespoon icing sugar
300ml thickened cream

1 Combine the water, sago and soda in medium bowl; cover, stand overnight.
2 Preheat oven to 180°C/160°C fan-forced. Grease eight ¾-cup (180ml) ovenproof moulds.
3 Beat butter, extract, sugar and egg in small bowl with electric mixer until light and fluffy. Stir in combined sifted flour and extra soda, sago mixture, breadcrumbs and sultanas.
4 Divide mixture among moulds; cover tightly with foil. Place moulds in baking dish; pour enough boiling water into baking dish to come halfway up sides of moulds. Bake 3 hours, topping up water level with boiling water during cooking.
5 Meanwhile, make orange cream.
6 Turn puddings into serving bowls; serve with orange cream.

orange cream Beat ingredients in small bowl with electric mixer until soft peaks form.

serves 8
preparation time 10 minutes
(plus standing time)
cooking time 3 hours
tip You can use Cointreau, Grand Marnier, Curaçao or any other orange-flavoured liqueur in this recipe.

sticky date cake with butterscotch sauce

3¾ cups (635g) dried
  seeded dates
3 cups (750ml) hot water
2 teaspoons bicarbonate
  of soda
185g butter, chopped
2¼ cups (500g) firmly packed
  brown sugar
6 eggs
3 cups (450g) self-raising flour
½ cup (60g) coarsely chopped
  walnuts
½ cup (60g) coarsely chopped
  pecans
butterscotch sauce
2 cups (440g) firmly packed
  brown sugar
500ml thickened cream
250g butter, chopped

1 Preheat oven to 180°C/160°C fan-forced. Grease 26cm x 36cm baking dish; double-line base and long sides with baking paper, bringing paper 5cm above edges of dish.

2 Combine dates and the water in medium saucepan; bring to the boil. Remove from heat; stir in soda. Stand 5 minutes. Blend or process date mixture until smooth.

3 Beat butter and sugar in large bowl with electric mixer until light and fluffy. Add eggs, one at a time, beating until combined between each addition. Stir in date mixture and flour; spread mixture into dish, sprinkle with nuts.

4 Bake, uncovered, in oven about 50 minutes. Stand cake in dish 10 minutes; turn, top-side up, onto wire rack.

5 Meanwhile, make butterscotch sauce.

6 Brush surface of hot cake with ⅓ cup of the hot butterscotch sauce. Serve with remaining sauce.

butterscotch sauce Stir ingredients in medium saucepan over heat, without boiling, until sugar dissolves; bring to the boil. Reduce heat; simmer 3 minutes.

serves 20
preparation time 20 minutes
cooking time 55 minutes
tips Cake is suitable to freeze. To defrost, wrap in foil and reheat in moderately slow oven for 20 minutes. The sauce is suitable to microwave.

vanilla panna cotta with berry jelly

120g raspberries
½ teaspoon gelatine
1½ tablespoons caster sugar
1 tablespoon lemon juice
⅓ cup (80ml) cranberry juice
vanilla panna cotta
2 teaspoons gelatine
¼ cup (55g) caster sugar
⅔ cup (160ml) milk
300ml thickened cream
½ teaspoon vanilla extract

1 Grease four ⅔-cup (160ml) metal moulds. Place four raspberries in each mould; reserve remaining raspberries.

2 Sprinkle gelatine and sugar over combined juices in small heatproof jug; stand jug in small saucepan of simmering water, stirring until gelatine and sugar dissolve.

3 Divide gelatine mixture among moulds, cover; refrigerate about 2 hours or until set.

4 Meanwhile, make vanilla panna cotta.

5 Gently pour cooled panna cotta into moulds, cover; refrigerate 3 hours or overnight.

6 Turn panna cotta onto serving plates; serve with remaining raspberries.

vanilla panna cotta Sprinkle gelatine and sugar over combined milk and cream in small saucepan. Stir over low heat, without boiling, until gelatine and sugar dissolve; stir in extract. Strain mixture into medium jug; cool panna cotta to room temperature.

serves 4
preparation time 20 minutes
(plus refrigeration time)
cooking time 15 minutes

mango bombe alaska

2 litres mango ice-cream,
softened
¼ cup (60ml) orange juice
2 tablespoons orange-flavoured
liqueur
16cm-round unfilled packaged
sponge cake
1 large mango (600g),
sliced thinly
4 egg whites
1 cup (220g) caster sugar

1 Line 15cm 1.375-litre (5½-cup) pudding basin or bowl with plastic wrap, extending plastic 5cm over edge of basin.

2 Pack ice-cream into basin, cover with foil; freeze about 2 hours or until firm.

3 Preheat oven to 240°C/220°C fan-forced.

4 Combine juice and liqueur in small jug. Trim top of cake to make level; split cake in half horizontally through centre. Place bottom layer of cake on oven tray; brush with half of the juice mixture. Top with mango, then with remaining cake half; brush with remaining juice mixture.

5 Invert ice-cream from pudding basin onto cake. Working quickly, trim cake to exact size of ice-cream; return to freezer.

6 Beat egg whites in small bowl with electric mixer until soft peaks form; gradually add sugar, beating until sugar dissolves between additions.

7 Remove bombe from freezer; spread meringue over to enclose bombe completely. Bake, uncovered, about 3 minutes or until browned lightly. Lift bombe alaska onto serving plate; serve immediately.

serves 6
preparation time 20 minutes
(plus freezing time)
cooking time 5 minutes
tips If mango ice-cream is unavailable, place canned drained mango slices and scoops of vanilla ice-cream alternately into the pudding basin.
You can use Cointreau, Grand Marnier, Curaçao or any other orange-flavoured liqueur in this recipe.

baked plums with frozen almond cream

Frozen almond cream is best made a day ahead.

16 ripe medium plums (1.8kg)
1 vanilla bean
½ cup (125ml) dry red wine
½ cup (110g) caster sugar
frozen almond cream
600ml thickened cream
¼ cup (40g) icing sugar
½ teaspoon vanilla extract
150g almond nougat,
    chopped finely
½ cup (80g) roasted almonds,
    chopped finely

1 Make frozen almond cream.
2 Preheat oven to 180°C/160°C fan-forced.
3 Cut a shallow cross in base of each plum; place plums, cut-side up, in single layer, in large shallow baking dish. Split vanilla bean in half lengthways; add to dish.
4 Pour wine over plums; sprinkle plums with sugar. Bake, uncovered, about 30 minutes or until plums are tender, brushing plums with juices halfway through cooking time. Discard vanilla bean.
5 Meanwhile, stand frozen almond cream at room temperature for 10 minutes.
6 Serve plums with frozen almond cream.
frozen almond cream Line 14cm x 21cm loaf pan with plastic wrap. Beat cream, sugar and extract in small bowl with electric mixer until soft peaks form; gently fold in nougat and nuts. Spread mixture into pan, cover with foil; freeze overnight.

serves 8
preparation time 20 minutes (plus freezing time)
cooking time 30 minutes
tip Separate pieces of nougat before folding into cream mixture to prevent them from clumping together.

wendy's sponge cake

4 eggs
¾ cup (165g) caster sugar
⅔ cup (100g) wheaten
  cornflour
¼ cup (30g) custard powder
1 teaspoon cream of tartar
½ teaspoon bicarbonate
  of soda
300ml thickened cream
1 tablespoon icing sugar
½ teaspoon vanilla extract
¼ cup (80g) strawberry jam,
  warmed
250g strawberries,
  sliced thinly
1 tablespoon icing sugar, extra

1 Preheat oven to 180°C/160°C fan-forced. Grease and flour two deep 22cm-round cake pans.

2 Beat eggs and caster sugar in small bowl with electric mixer about 5 minutes or until thick and creamy; transfer to large bowl.

3 Sift dry ingredients twice onto paper, then sift over egg mixture; gently fold together.

4 Divide mixture evenly between pans; bake, uncovered, about 20 minutes. Turn sponges immediately onto baking-paper-lined wire rack; turn top-side up to cool.

5 Beat cream, sifted icing sugar and extract in small bowl with electric mixer until firm peaks form. Place one sponge on serving plate; spread with jam, then with cream mixture. Top with strawberry slices, then with remaining sponge. Dust with sifted extra icing sugar.

serves 10
preparation time 20 minutes
cooking time 20 minutes
tip When folding flour into egg mixture, you can use a large metal spoon, a rubber spatula or a whisk, or use one hand like a rake.

italian ricotta cheesecake

1kg ricotta cheese
5 eggs, beaten lightly
1 tablespoon finely grated
    lemon rind
¼ cup (60ml) lemon juice
½ teaspoon vanilla extract
1 cup (220g) caster sugar
¼ cup (40g) sultanas
½ cup (125g) finely chopped
    mixed glacé fruit
pastry
90g butter, softened
1 egg
¼ cup (55g) caster sugar
1¼ cups (185g) plain flour
¼ cup (35g) self-raising flour

1 Make pastry.
2 Reduce oven temperature to 160°C/140°C fan-forced.
3 Blend or process cheese, eggs, rind, juice, extract and sugar until smooth. Stir in sultanas and glacé fruit; pour cheesecake filling over pastry base.
4 Bake cheesecake, uncovered, about 50 minutes or until filling sets; cool to room temperature, then refrigerate until cold.

pastry Grease 25cm springform tin. Beat butter in small bowl with electric mixer until smooth; add egg and sugar, beating until just combined. Stir in half of the combined sifted flours; work remaining flour in by hand. Knead pastry gently on floured surface until smooth. Cover with plastic wrap; refrigerate 30 minutes. Roll pastry between sheets of baking paper until large enough to cover base of tin. Lift pastry into tin; press into base. Lightly prick pastry with fork; cover, refrigerate 30 minutes. Meanwhile, preheat oven to 200°C/180°C fan-forced. Bake pastry, uncovered, 20 minutes.

serves 16
preparation time 30 minutes
(plus refrigeration and cooling time)
cooking time 1 hour 10 minutes
tip This recipe is best made a day ahead and stored, covered, in the refrigerator overnight.

pavlova

4 egg whites
1 cup (220g) caster sugar
1 tablespoon cornflour
1 teaspoon white vinegar
300ml thickened cream
1 teaspoon vanilla extract
1 tablespoon icing sugar
150g strawberries, sliced thinly
150g blueberries
120g raspberries

1 Preheat oven to 120°C/100°C fan-forced. Grease and line oven tray with baking paper; trace an 18cm circle on paper.
2 Beat egg whites in small bowl with electric mixer until soft peaks form. Gradually add caster sugar, a tablespoon at a time, beating until sugar dissolves between additions. Fold in cornflour and vinegar.
3 Spread meringue inside circle on tray; level top with spatula. Bake, uncovered, about 1¼ hours or until meringue is firm. Cool meringue in oven with door ajar.
4 Beat cream, extract and sifted icing sugar in small bowl with electric mixer until soft peaks form. Serve meringue topped with cream mixture and fruit.

serves 8
preparation time 20 minutes (plus cooling time)
cooking time 1 hour 15 minutes
tips If you prefer not to accompany the pavlova with berries, you can use kiwifruit, thinly sliced pineapple, pawpaw and passionfruit pulp. Pavlova meringue can be made up to four days ahead, then topped with cream mixture and fruit up to one hour before serving.

white-choc panna cotta
with passionfruit sauce

*Sauternes is a dessert wine
from the region of the same
name in western France.
You will need approximately
six passionfruit for this recipe.*

300ml thickened cream
¾ cup (180ml) milk
150g white eating chocolate,
    chopped coarsely
⅓ cup (75g) caster sugar
2 teaspoons gelatine
1 tablespoon water
½ cup (125ml)
    passionfruit pulp
1 cup (250ml) Sauternes-style
    dessert wine

1 Grease six ½-cup (125ml) non-metallic moulds.

2 Combine cream, milk, chocolate and 2 tablespoons of the sugar in small saucepan; stir over heat, without boiling, until smooth.

3 Sprinkle gelatine over the water in small heatproof jug. Stand jug in small saucepan of simmering water; stir until gelatine dissolves. Stir into cream mixture.

4 Divide mixture among moulds; refrigerate, covered, about 3 hours or until set.

5 Meanwhile, combine passionfruit, wine and remaining sugar in small saucepan; bring to the boil. Reduce heat; simmer, uncovered, without stirring, about 10 minutes or until passionfruit syrup reduces by a third; cool.

6 Turn panna cotta onto serving plates; drizzle with passionfruit syrup.

serves 6
preparation time 20 minutes
(plus refrigeration time)
cooking time 10 minutes
tips Panna cotta translates from Italian as "cooked cream". It can be made a day ahead and refrigerated, covered.
Serve the remaining dessert wine with the panna cotta, if you like.

chocolate hazelnut self-saucing puddings

Nutella is a commercial spread made of milk chocolate and hazelnuts.

½ cup (125ml) milk
40g dark eating chocolate, chopped coarsely
50g butter
⅓ cup (35g) cocoa powder
½ cup (75g) self-raising flour
¼ cup (25g) hazelnut meal
⅓ cup (75g) caster sugar
⅔ cup (150g) firmly packed brown sugar
1 egg, beaten lightly
¾ cup (180ml) water
40g butter, chopped, extra
200g vanilla ice-cream
chocolate hazelnut sauce
½ cup (125ml) cream
2 tablespoons brown sugar
50g dark eating chocolate, chopped finely
⅓ cup (110g) Nutella
1 tablespoon Frangelico

1 Preheat oven to 180°C/160°C fan-forced. Grease four 1-cup (250ml) ovenproof dishes.
2 Stir milk, chocolate, butter and half the cocoa in small saucepan over low heat until smooth.
3 Combine flour, hazelnut meal, caster sugar and half the brown sugar in medium bowl. Add chocolate mixture and egg; stir until combined. Divide mixture among dishes.
4 Stir the water, extra butter, remaining brown sugar and remaining cocoa in small saucepan over low heat until smooth. Pour hot mixture gently and evenly over puddings; bake puddings, uncovered, in oven about 25 minutes.
5 Meanwhile, make chocolate hazelnut sauce.
6 Stand puddings 5 minutes; top with ice-cream then chocolate hazelnut sauce.

chocolate hazelnut sauce Combine cream and sugar in small saucepan; bring to the boil. Remove from heat; add chocolate, stir until smooth. Add Nutella and the liqueur; stir until smooth.

serves 4
preparation time 15 minutes
cooking time 25 minutes
tips This dessert is best served hot because the sauce is quickly absorbed by the puddings. Frangelico is a hazelnut-flavoured liqueur.

passionfruit and coconut crème brûlée

You will need six passionfruit for this recipe.

2 eggs
4 egg yolks
¼ cup (55g) caster sugar
½ cup (125ml) passionfruit
  pulp
1⅔ cups (400ml) coconut cream
300ml thickened cream
2 tablespoons brown sugar

1 Preheat oven to 180°C/160°C fan-forced.

2 Combine eggs, egg yolks, caster sugar and passionfruit pulp in medium heatproof bowl.

3 Combine coconut cream and cream in small saucepan; bring to the boil. Gradually whisk hot cream mixture into egg mixture. Place bowl over medium saucepan of simmering water; stir over heat about 10 minutes or until custard mixture thickens slightly and coats the back of a spoon.

4 Divide custard among eight ½-cup (125ml) heatproof dishes or cups. Place dishes in large baking dish. Pour enough boiling water into baking dish to come halfway up sides of dishes; bake in oven about 20 minutes or until custards just set. Remove custards from water; cool to room temperature. Cover; refrigerate 3 hours or overnight.

5 Preheat grill. Place custards in shallow flameproof dish filled with ice cubes; sprinkle each with 1 teaspoon brown sugar. Using finger, spread the sugar evenly over surface of each custard, pressing in gently; place under hot grill until tops are caramelised.

serves 8
preparation time 15 minutes
(plus cooling and refrigeration time)
cooking time 40 minutes
tip Preheat grill on highest setting for about 5 minutes. It's important the sugar on the custards browns as quickly as possible (the ice in the baking dish helps keep the custards cold while the sugar is caramelising).

margarita mousse

¼ cup (55g) white sugar
1 tablespoon gelatine
2 tablespoons water
1 cup (220g) caster sugar
1¼ cups (300g) sour cream
300ml thickened cream
½ cup (120g) spreadable
   cream cheese
green food colouring
¼ cup (60ml) tequila
1 tablespoon orange-flavoured
   liqueur
1 teaspoon finely grated
   lime rind
¾ cup (180ml) lime juice
⅓ cup (80ml) orange juice

1 Place white sugar on saucer. Dip rims of six ¾-cup (180ml) glasses in bowl of cold water then into white sugar; refrigerate glasses.
2 Sprinkle gelatine over the water in small heatproof jug; stand jug in small saucepan of simmering water. Stir until gelatine dissolves; cool 5 minutes.
3 Beat caster sugar, sour cream, cream and cream cheese in medium bowl with electric mixer until sugar dissolves and mixture is fluffy. Beat in enough colouring to tint mixture a pale green.
4 Whisk tequila, liqueur, rind, juices and gelatine mixture into cream mixture. Divide mixture among glasses; refrigerate about 2 hours or until mousse sets.

serves 6
preparation time 20 minutes
(plus refrigeration time)
cooking time 5 minutes
tips Mousse can be made a day ahead and refrigerated, covered, until ready to serve. Gelatine mixture should be cool but not set, and should be approximately the same temperature as the cream mixture when they're combined; if not, the mousse can split into layers or become rubbery.
You can use Cointreau, Grand Marnier, Curaçao or any other orange-flavoured liqueur in this recipe.

vanilla bean ice-cream
with choc-almond crunch

2 egg yolks
⅓ cup (75g) caster sugar
1 cup (250ml) milk
300ml thickened cream
1 vanilla bean, split in half
   lengthways
choc-almond crunch
2 cups (440g) caster sugar
1 cup (250ml) water
200g dark eating chocolate,
   chopped coarsely
½ cup (40g) flaked
   almonds, roasted

serves 6
preparation time 20 minutes
(plus freezing time)
cooking time 20 minutes
tip Milk chocolate can
be used instead of dark
chocolate, if preferred.

1 Whisk egg yolks and sugar in medium bowl until light and fluffy.

2 Combine milk and cream in medium saucepan. Scrape seeds from vanilla bean; add bean and seeds to pan. Bring milk mixture almost to the boil.

3 Remove milk mixture from heat; discard vanilla bean. Whisking constantly, gradually pour milk mixture into egg mixture. Return custard mixture to same saucepan; cook over low heat, stirring constantly, until mixture begins to thicken and coats the back of a spoon (do not boil or mixture will curdle).

4 Return custard to same medium bowl. Cover surface completely with plastic wrap; freeze about 4 hours or until ice-cream is firm.

5 Meanwhile, make choc-almond crunch.

6 Line 8cm x 25cm bar cake pan with plastic wrap. Blend or process ice-cream until smooth; spread into pan. Cover with foil; freeze until firm. Turn ice-cream out of pan; cut into 12 slices. Serve with shards of choc-almond crunch.

choc-almond crunch Combine sugar and the water in medium heavy-based saucepan; stir over low heat until sugar dissolves. Bring to the boil. Boil, uncovered, without stirring, about 10 minutes or until syrup is a deep golden colour. Pour toffee mixture into 20cm x 30cm lamington pan; stand 5 minutes. Sprinkle chocolate over hot toffee, spreading with a palette knife to completely cover toffee. Sprinkle with nuts; refrigerate until set. Break choc-almond crunch into shards.

fig and brioche pudding

Brioche, a rich, yeast-risen French bread made with butter and eggs, is available from pâtisseries or better bakeries.

1½ cups (375ml) milk
600ml cream
1 cinnamon stick
1 vanilla bean
¼ cup (90g) honey
4 eggs
2 small brioche (200g)
3 medium fresh figs (180g)
1 tablespoon demerara sugar

1 Preheat oven to 180°C/160°C fan-forced. Grease shallow 2-litre (8 cup) ovenproof dish.
2 Stir milk, cream, cinnamon, vanilla bean and honey in medium saucepan until hot; strain into large heatproof jug.
3 Whisk eggs in large bowl; whisking constantly, pour hot milk mixture into egg mixture.
4 Cut each brioche into six slices and each fig into five slices. Layer brioche and figs, overlapping slightly, in dish. Pour hot milk mixture over brioche and figs; sprinkle with sugar.
5 Place pudding dish in large baking dish; add enough boiling water to come halfway up sides of dish. Bake, uncovered, in oven about 40 minutes or until pudding sets. Remove pudding dish from baking dish; stand 5 minutes before serving.

serves 6
preparation time 15 minutes
cooking time 1 hour 15 minutes
tips Remove pudding from water bath immediately after cooking to prevent it from overcooking.
A whole vanilla bean can be rinsed under warm water, dried, then stored in an airtight jar for future use.
If you cannot find demerara sugar, use white sugar in its place.

flourless hazelnut chocolate cake

Hazelnut meal replaces the flour in this recipe.

⅓ cup (35g) cocoa powder
⅓ cup (80ml) hot water
150g dark eating chocolate, melted
150g butter, melted
1⅓ cups (275g) firmly packed brown sugar
1 cup (125g) hazelnut meal
4 eggs, separated
1 tablespoon cocoa powder, extra

1 Preheat oven to 180°C/160°C fan-forced. Grease deep 19cm-square cake pan; line base and sides with baking paper.

2 Blend cocoa with the hot water in large bowl until smooth. Stir in chocolate, butter, sugar, hazelnut meal and egg yolks.

3 Beat egg whites in small bowl with electric mixer until soft peaks form; fold into chocolate mixture in two batches.

4 Pour mixture into pan; bake about 1 hour or until firm. Stand cake 15 minutes before turning, top-side up, onto wire rack to cool. Dust with sifted extra cocoa to serve.

serves 9
preparation time 20 minutes (plus standing time)
cooking time 1 hour
tip This cake can be made up to four days ahead and refrigerated, covered. It can also be frozen for up to three months.
Hazelnut meal, also sold as ground hazelnuts, is a flour-like substance made after the nuts have been roasted.

choc-cherry ice-cream timbale

Cherry Ripe is a chocolate
bar filled with coconut and
glacé cherries.

2 litres (8 cups) vanilla
    ice-cream
2 x 85g Cherry Ripe bars,
    chopped coarsely
1 cup (140g) vienna almonds,
    chopped coarsely
50g pink marshmallows,
    chopped coarsely
50g dark eating chocolate,
    chopped coarsely
pink food colouring
300ml cream
100g white eating chocolate,
    chopped finely

1 Soften ice-cream in large bowl; stir in
Cherry Ripe, nuts, marshmallow, dark
chocolate and enough colouring to tint the
ice-cream pink. Divide mixture among eight
1-cup (250ml) moulds. Cover with foil; freeze
3 hours or overnight.
2 Place cream in small saucepan; bring to the
boil. Remove from heat; add white chocolate.
Stir until chocolate melts.
3 Turn ice-cream timbales onto serving plates;
drizzle with warm white chocolate sauce.

serves 8
preparation time 10 minutes
(plus freezing time)
cooking time 2 minutes
tips Use a good quality ice-cream; actual
varieties of ice-cream differ from manufacturer
to manufacturer depending on the quantities
of air and fat incorporated into the mixture.
Almonds coated in a toffee mixture are called
vienna almonds; scorched almonds can be
used instead.

mixed berry cake with vanilla bean syrup

125g butter, chopped
1 cup (220g) caster sugar
3 eggs
½ cup (75g) plain flour
¼ cup (35g) self-raising flour
½ cup (60g) almond meal
⅓ cup (80g) sour cream
1½ cups (225g)
   frozen mixed berries
½ cup (100g) drained canned
   seeded black cherries
vanilla bean syrup
½ cup (125ml) water
½ cup (110g) caster sugar
2 vanilla beans

1 Preheat oven to 180°C/160°C fan-forced. Grease 20cm baba pan thoroughly.
2 Beat butter and sugar in small bowl with electric mixer until light and fluffy. Add eggs, one at a time, beating until just combined between additions. (Mixture may curdle at this stage but will come together later.)
3 Transfer mixture to large bowl; stir in sifted flours, almond meal, sour cream, berries and cherries. Pour mixture into pan; bake, uncovered, about 40 minutes.
4 Meanwhile, make vanilla bean syrup.
5 Stand cake 5 minutes; turn onto wire rack placed over a large tray. Pour hot vanilla bean syrup over hot cake.
vanilla bean syrup Combine the water and sugar in small saucepan. Split vanilla beans in half lengthways; scrape seeds into pan then place pods in pan. Stir over heat, without boiling, until sugar dissolves. Simmer, uncovered, without stirring, 5 minutes. Using tongs, remove pods from syrup.

serves 8
preparation time 20 minutes
cooking time 40 minutes

chocolate butterscotch cake

¼ cup (25g) cocoa powder
1¼ cups (185g)
   self-raising flour
250g butter, softened
1 cup (200g) firmly packed
   dark brown sugar
2 eggs
1 tablespoon golden syrup
½ cup (125ml) milk
mascarpone cream
250g mascarpone cheese
300ml thickened cream
caramel icing
60g butter
½ cup (100g) firmly packed
   dark brown sugar
¼ cup (60ml) milk
1½ cups (240g) icing sugar

1 Preheat oven to 180°C/160°C fan-forced. Grease deep 20cm-round cake pan; line base and side with baking paper.

2 Sift cocoa and flour into large bowl; add remaining ingredients. Beat with electric mixer on low speed until combined. Increase speed to medium; beat until mixture has just changed in colour. Pour mixture into pan; bake about 1 hour. Stand cake 10 minutes; turn, top-side up, onto wire rack to cool.

3 Meanwhile, make mascarpone cream; make caramel icing.

4 Using large serrated knife, split cake into three layers. Centre one layer on serving plate; spread with a third of the mascarpone cream and a third of the caramel icing. Repeat with second layer and half of the remaining mascarpone cream and half of the remaining caramel icing; top with remaining cake layer. Cover top cake layer with remaining mascarpone cream then drizzle with remaining caramel icing; swirl for marbled effect. Refrigerate about 30 minutes or until icing is firm.

mascarpone cream Whisk ingredients in small bowl until soft peaks form.

caramel icing Heat butter, brown sugar and milk in small saucepan, stirring constantly, without boiling, until sugar dissolves; remove from heat. Add icing sugar; stir until smooth.

serves 10
preparation time 20 minutes
(plus refrigeration time)
cooking time 1 hour
tip Do not overbeat the mascarpone cream mixture as it could curdle.

whole tangelo cake

Tangelos are a cross between a grapefruit and a tangerine, tasting more like the latter but closer in size to the former. You need four tangelos for this recipe. Any citrus fruit of similar size can be substituted for the tangelo.

2 medium tangelos (420g)
125g butter, chopped
1½ cups (330g) caster sugar
2 eggs
1 cup (150g) self-raising flour
½ cup (75g) plain flour
½ cup (45g) desiccated
  coconut
tangelo syrup
1 cup (220g) caster sugar
rind of 1 tangelo, sliced thinly
⅔ cup (160ml) tangelo juice
⅓ cup (80ml) water

1 Place tangelos in medium saucepan; cover with cold water. Bring to the boil; drain. Repeat process two more times; cool to room temperature.

2 Preheat oven to 180°C/160°C fan-forced. Grease deep 22cm-round cake pan; line base and side with baking paper.

3 Halve tangelos; discard seeds. Blend or process tangelo until pulpy; transfer to large bowl.

4 Beat butter, sugar and eggs together in small bowl with electric mixer until light and fluffy. Add butter mixture to tangelo pulp; stir until combined.

5 Stir in sifted flours with coconut; pour mixture into pan. Bake about 45 minutes.

6 Meanwhile, make tangelo syrup.

7 Stand cake 5 minutes before turning, top-side up, onto wire rack over tray. Pour hot tangelo syrup over hot cake. Return any syrup that drips onto tray into jug; pour over cake. Serve cake warm.

tangelo syrup Using wooden spoon, stir ingredients in small saucepan over heat, without boiling, until sugar dissolves; bring to the boil. Reduce heat; simmer, uncovered, without stirring, 2 minutes. Pour into medium heatproof jug.

serves 16
preparation time 20 minutes
(plus cooling time)
cooking time 45 minutes

glossary

baking powder a raising agent consisting mainly of two parts cream of tartar to one part bicarbonate of soda (baking soda).

bicarbonate of soda carb or baking soda.

breadcrumbs
  fresh usually white bread processed into crumbs.
  stale crumbs made by blending or processing one or two-day-old bread.

butter use salted or unsalted (sweet) butter; 125g is equal to one stick of butter.

cheese
  mascarpone a fresh cultured-cream product made in much the same way as yogurt. Whiteish to creamy yellow in colour, with a soft, rich, creamy, spreadable texture.
  ricotta a soft, sweet, moist, white cow-milk cheese.

chocolate
  chocolate Melts small discs of compounded milk, white or dark chocolate ideal for melting and moulding.
  dark eating also known as semi-sweet or luxury chocolate.
  milk most popular eating chocolate; mild and sweet.
  white eating very sensitive to heat so is not good for cooking.

cinnamon dried inner bark of the shoots of the cinnamon tree; available in stick or ground form.

cocoa powder also known as unsweetened cocoa; fermented, roasted, shelled, and ground cocoa beans.

coconut
  desiccated concentrated, dried, unsweetened, finely shredded coconut flesh.
  shredded sweetened thin strips of dried coconut flesh.

corella pears miniature dessert pear up to 10cm long. Any firm pear can be substituted.

cornflour also known as cornstarch. Available made from corn or wheat.

cream
  cheese commonly known as Philadelphia or Philly, a soft cow-milk cheese; sold at supermarkets.
  crème fraîche mature fermented cream having a slightly tangy, nutty flavour and velvety texture.
  sour a thick commercially-cultured soured cream.
  thickened a whipping cream containing a thickener.

custard powder instant mixture used to make pouring custard; similar to North American instant pudding mixes.

flour
  plain also known as all-purpose flour.
  self-raising all-purpose plain flour with baking powder added in the proportion of 1 cup flour to 2 teaspoons baking powder.

gelatine a setting agent; we used powdered gelatine. It is also available in sheet form, known as leaf gelatine. Two teaspoons of powdered gelatine (7g or one sachet) is roughly equivalent to four gelatine leaves.

ginger, ground also known as powdered ginger; cannot be substituted for fresh ginger.

glacé fruit preserved in sugar syrup.

golden syrup a by-product of refined sugarcane; pure maple syrup or honey can be substituted.

jam also known as preserve or conserve; a thickened mixture of fruit and sugar.

lamington pan 20cm x 30cm slab cake pan, 3cm deep.

maple syrup distilled from the sap of maple trees. Maple-flavoured syrup or pancake syrup is not an adequate substitute for the real thing.

marmalade a preserve, usually based on citrus fruit and its rind, cooked with sugar until the mixture has an intense flavour and thick consistency.

meal nuts ground into a coarse flour texture.

mixed dried fruit a mix of sultanas, raisins, currants, mixed peel and cherries.

mixed spice generally contains caraway, allspice, coriander, cumin, nutmeg and ginger.

nutmeg the dried nut of an evergreen tree; available ground, or you can grate your own with a fine grater.

nuts

almonds flat, pointy-tipped nuts having a pitted brown shell enclosing a creamy white kernel that is covered by a brown skin. *Flaked almonds* are paper-thin slices; *slivered* are small lengthways-cut pieces.

brazil a triangular nut with a rich, mild white flesh encased with a brown skin.

hazelnuts also known as filberts; plump, grape-size, rich, sweet nut having a brown inedible skin that is removed by rubbing heated nuts together vigorously in a tea towel.

macadamia rich, buttery nut; store in refrigerator because of high oil content.

pecans golden-brown, buttery, rich nut.

pine also known as pignoli; not in fact a nut, but a small, cream-coloured kernel from pine cones.

pistachio green, delicately flavoured nut inside hard off-white shells. To peel, soak shelled nuts in boiling water for about 5 minutes; drain, then pat dry with absorbent paper. Rub skins with cloth to peel.

walnuts rich and flavourful fruit of the walnut tree; high in fat, so keep refrigerated.

pastry

fillo also known as phyllo or filo; tissue-thin pastry sheets purchased chilled or frozen.

ready-rolled puff packaged sheets of frozen puff pastry; available from supermarkets.

sago also known as seed or pearl tapioca; comes from the sago palm and is used in soups and desserts and as a thickening agent.

quince yellow-skinned fruit with hard texture and astringent, tart taste; eaten cooked or as a preserve.

liqueur

crème de cacao chocolate-flavoured liqueur, often scented with vanilla. *Dark crème de cacao* is dark brown, while *white crème de cacao* is a clear, colourless form. If a recipe calls for just crème de cacao, use the white version.

cointreau citrus-flavoured liqueur.

framboise raspberry-flavoured liqueur.

frangelico hazelnut-flavoured liqueur.

grand marnier orange-flavoured liqueur.

irish cream we used Baileys, a smooth and creamy natural blend of fresh Irish cream, spirits, whisky, cocoa and vanilla.

kahlua coffee-flavoured liqueur.

malibu coconut-flavoured rum.

rum we use dark underproof rum (not overproof) for a more subtle flavour. White rum is colourless rum; we use Bacardi.

tequila colourless liqueur made from the fermented sap of a desert plant.

sugar

brown soft, finely granulated sugar retaining molasses for its colour and flavour.

caster also known as finely granulated or superfine table sugar.

demerara small golden-coloured crystal sugar.

icing also known as confectioners' or powdered sugar; granulated sugar crushed together with a small amount of cornflour.

palm also known as nam tan pip, jaggery, jawa or gula melaka. Usually sold in rock-hard cakes; substitute with brown sugar.

pure icing also known as confectioners' sugar or powdered sugar.

white also known as crystal or granulated table sugar.

sultanas dried grapes, also known as golden raisins.

vanilla

bean dried long, thin pod of a tropical golden orchid; the minuscule black seeds inside the bean impart a luscious vanilla flavour.

extract made by extracting the flavour from the vanilla bean pod.

conversion chart

MEASURES

One Australian metric measuring cup holds approximately 250ml, one Australian metric tablespoon holds 20ml, one Australian metric teaspoon holds 5ml.

The difference between one country's measuring cups and another's is within a 2- or 3-teaspoon variance, and will not affect your cooking results. North America, New Zealand and the United Kingdom use a 15ml tablespoon. All cup and spoon measurements are level. The most accurate way of measuring dry ingredients is to weigh them. When measuring liquids, use a clear glass or plastic jug with metric markings.

We use large eggs with an average weight of 60g.

DRY MEASURES

METRIC	IMPERIAL
15g	½oz
30g	1oz
60g	2oz
90g	3oz
125g	4oz (¼lb)
155g	5oz
185g	6oz
220g	7oz
250g	8oz (½lb)
280g	9oz
315g	10oz
345g	11oz
375g	12oz (¾lb)
410g	13oz
440g	14oz
470g	15oz
500g	16oz (1lb)
750g	24oz (1½lb)
1kg	32oz (2lb)

LIQUID MEASURES

METRIC	IMPERIAL
30ml	1 fluid oz
60ml	2 fluid oz
100ml	3 fluid oz
125ml	4 fluid oz
150ml	5 fluid oz (¼ pint/1 gill)
190ml	6 fluid oz
250ml	8 fluid oz
300ml	10 fluid oz (½ pint)
500ml	16 fluid oz
600ml	20 fluid oz (1 pint)
1000ml (1 litre)	1¾ pints

LENGTH MEASURES

METRIC	IMPERIAL
3mm	⅛in
6mm	¼in
1cm	½in
2cm	¾in
2.5cm	1in
5cm	2in
6cm	2½in
8cm	3in
10cm	4in
13cm	5in
15cm	6in
18cm	7in
20cm	8in
23cm	9in
25cm	10in
28cm	11in
30cm	12in (1ft)

OVEN TEMPERATURES

These oven temperatures are only a guide for conventional ovens. For fan-forced ovens, check the manufacturer's manual.

	°C (CELSIUS)	°F (FAHRENHEIT)	GAS MARK
Very slow	120	250	½
Slow	150	275 – 300	1 – 2
Moderately slow	160	325	3
Moderate	180	350 – 375	4 – 5
Moderately hot	200	400	6
Hot	220	425 – 450	7 – 8
Very hot	240	475	9

index

Are you missing some of the world's favourite cookbooks?

The Australian Women's Weekly cookbooks are available from bookshops, cookshops, supermarkets and other stores all over the world. You can also buy direct from the publisher, using the order form below.

MINI SERIES £3.50 190x138MM 64 PAGES

TITLE	QTY	TITLE	QTY	TITLE	QTY
4 Fast Ingredients		Healthy Everyday Food 4 Kids		Simple Slices	
4 Kids to Cook		Ice-creams & Sorbets		Simply Seafood	
15-minute Feasts		Indian Cooking		Soup plus	
50 Fast Chicken Fillets		Italian Favourites		Spanish Favourites	
50 Fast Desserts		Indonesian Favourites		Stir-fries	
Biscuits, Brownies & Bisottti		Jams & Jellies		Stir-fry Favourites	
Bites		Japanese Favourites		Summer Salads	
Bowl Food		Kebabs & Skewers		Tagines & Couscous	
Burgers, Rösti & Fritters		Kids Party Food		Tapas, Antipasto & Mezze	
Cafe Cakes		Lebanese Cooking		Tarts	
Cafe Food		Low-Fat Delicious		Tex-Mex	
Casseroles & Curries		Low Fat Fast		Thai Favourites	
Char-grills & Barbecues		Malaysian Favourites		The Fast Egg	
Cheesecakes, Pavlova & Trifles		Mince Favourites		The Young Chef	
Chinese Favourites		Muffins		Vegetarian	
Chocolate Cakes		Noodles & Stir-fries		Vegie Main Meals	
Crumbles & Bakes		Old-Fashioned Desserts		Vietnamese Favourites	
Cupcakes & Cookies		Outdoor Eating			
Dips & Dippers		Packed Lunch			
Dried Fruit & Nuts		Party Food			
Drinks		Pickles and Chutneys			
Easy Pies & Pastries		Pasta			
Fast Fillets		Potatoes		TOTAL COST	£
Fishcakes & Crispybakes		Quick Desserts			
Gluten-free Cooking		Roast			
Grills & Barbecues		Salads			

Photocopy and complete coupon below

Name _____

Address _____

_____ Postcode _____

Country _____ Phone (business hours) _____

Email*(optional) _____

* By including your email address, you consent to receipt of any email regarding this magazine, and other emails which inform you of ACP's other publications, products, services and events, and to promote third party goods and services you may be interested in.

I enclose my cheque/money order for £ _____ or please charge £ _____ to my:

☐ Access ☐ Mastercard ☐ Visa ☐ Diners Club

Card number

3 digit security code *(found on reverse of card)* _____

Cardholder's signature _____ Expiry date ___ / ___

To order: Mail or fax – photocopy or complete the order form above, and send your credit card details or cheque payable to: Australian Consolidated Press (UK), 10 Scirocco Close, Moulton Park Office Village, Northampton NN3 6AP, phone (+44) (01) 604 642200, fax (+44) (01) 604 642300, e-mail books@acpuk.com or order online at www.acpuk.com

Non-UK residents: We accept the credit cards listed on the coupon, or cheques, drafts or International Money Orders payable in sterling and drawn on a UK bank. Credit card charges are at the exchange rate current at the time of payment. All pricing current at time of going to press and subject to change/availability.

Postage and packing UK: Add £1.00 per order plus 75p per book.

Postage and packing overseas: Add £2.00 per order plus £1.50 per book.